THE STORY
OF THE
STANCZAK BROTHERS
BASEBALL TEAM

★ ★ ★ ★ ★

BASEBALL'S ALL BROTHERS
WORLD CHAMPIONS

JOHN R. STANCZAK

Charleston, SC
www.PalmettoPublishing.com

The Story of the Stanczak Brothers Baseball Team
Copyright © 2021 by John R. Stanczak

All rights reserved

No portion of this book may be reproduced, stored in a retrieval system, or transmitted in any form by any means–electronic, mechanical, photocopy, recording, or other–except for brief quotations in printed reviews, without prior permission of the author.

Paperback ISBN: 978-1-63837-000-0

Dedication

This story has been waiting a long time to be told. It has been 100 years since the first of the Stanczak brothers threw his baseball mitt on the field that became their "field of dreams," a cow pasture near the family home.

I recently celebrated my 90th birthday, and I regret that I waited all these years to share this rich history with my family and friends. My children and grandchildren and the remaining descendants of the Stanczak All-Brothers baseball team – indeed anybody who enjoys a good baseball story – deserve to know the story of ten brothers who left their mark on our great American pastime.

I would be remiss if I failed to mention my younger brother Jim at the outset of this book. Jim and I long planned to collaborate in telling this story. Unfortunately, Jim died in 2018, after compiling much of the historical data about the brothers' story. In keeping with Stanczak family tradition, Jim was an exceptionally good baseball player. He starred on the Bradley University baseball team and played semi-pro baseball both before and after finishing college. It was often said that Jim had the sweetest left-hand swing in all of Lake County, and he could hit for power. He was offered contracts by several major league scouts; two such offers made at the family home just prior to Jim entering the U.S. Navy where he served as a Naval Aviator and attained the rank of Captain. His last Navy assignment was as commander of the Naval Air Station in Glenview, Illinois.

I regret that Jim and I were unable to finish this labor of love together, but I am hoping they have a library in heaven so Jim can enjoy the finished story together with our father and our uncles.

Acknowledgements

I am grateful for the contributions of my children that enabled me to complete this book. I want to thank my daughter Diana for her work transcribing my scribblings and turning pages and pages of handwritten scrawl into something readable. I thank my daughters Cheryl and Karen who helped me with my research and ensured that I did not stray too far from the facts . . . which is easy to do at my stage of life! Finally, I am grateful to my son, Steve, for restraining my occasionally over-the-top creative flourishes and for his wonderful job of performing the final edits and for doing whatever else was needed to help me in my quest to tell this wonderful story.

I also want to acknowledge the incredible support that I received throughout this journey from my life partner, Jo Gregory. She was a constant – and essential – source of encouragement during this long process.

TABLE OF CONTENTS

Foreword ·ix

Chapter 1 A New Life in America · · · · · · · · · · · · · · · · · 1

Chapter 2 A Baseball Team is Born · · · · · · · · · · · · · · · 5

Chapter 3 War Comes to North Chicago · · · · · · · · · · · 9

Chapter 4 Back to Baseball · 15

Chapter 5 A World Championship · · · · · · · · · · · · · · · · 30

Chapter 6 It Ain't Over 'Till the Fat Lady Sings · · · · · 37

Appendix: My Baseball Memories · · · · · · · · · · · · · · · · · 43

About the Author · 49

FOREWORD

According to information compiled by the National Baseball Hall of Fame, there were at one time or another 23 all-brother teams across the country. There were probably more. For instance, the Dieke Brothers team from the Texas Hill Country, which played the Stanczak Brothers in the All-Brothers Baseball Championship game on August 18, 1935, is not included on the Hall of Fame list. These teams flourished during the Great Depression when large families were common, and baseball offered one of the few respites from the gloomy economic conditions of the time.

John R. Stanczak

ALL-BROTHER BASEBALL TEAMS

The National Baseball Hall of Fame has identified 22 different all-brother baseball teams. These unique squads date from the 1860's, and they played at a variety of competitive levels. This list is organized by family name, and provides some basic information from our archival files. Additional details concerning these groups can be obtained by contacting the library reference desk (607-547-0330).

FAMILY NAME	HOMETOWN	ERA
Acerra (12 brothers)	Long Branch, NJ	1948
Birkenmeyer (10 brothers)	Wappingers Falls, NY	1906
Coombs (11 brothers)	Wichita Falls, TX	1932
Curleys (9 brothers)	Bridgeton, NJ	1930's
Flanagan (9 brothers)	Powhatan, VA	1920's
Frederickson (12 brothers)	Eidswold, MN	1920's
Gillum (9 brothers)	Madison Mills, VA	1912
Haas (9 brothers)	Napierville, IL	1930's
Karpen (unconfirmed)	Chicago, IL	1890
Ladouceur (9 brothers)	Ogenburg, NY	unknown
Lennon (9 brothers)	Joliet, IL	1891
Madden (9 brothers)	MA	unknown
Marlatt (11 brothers)	Hawk Springs, WY	1929
May (9 brothers)	Belfry, KY	1934 - early '40's
McEntee (8 brothers)	Rochester, NY	1890
Newell (9 brothers)	Plankington, SD	1930's
Simon (10 brothers)	Olsburg, KS	1927-1929
Skillicorn (9 brothers)	Watsonville, CA	1920's
Stanzak (10 brothers)	Wakegan, IL	1929
Thompson (9 brothers)	Winchester, NH	1869-1899
Van Tassel (9 brothers)	Westfield, PA	1902
Weir (9 brothers)	Cooperstown, NY	1937

Compiled by Virginia Reinholdt, National Baseball Hall of Fame Library (Oct. 1998)

The stories of these all-brother teams have been told in bits and pieces over the years, including many that referenced the greatest brothers team of them all: the Stanczak Brothers

The Story of the Stanczak Brothers Baseball Team

of North Chicago, Illinois. In my research I found several baseball books that included tales about the prowess of the Stanczak Brothers baseball team. I discovered numerous newspaper articles, copies of old advertising flyers, letters to semi-pro baseball organizations, and of course, information passed down from my dad, my uncles, my eldest brother, and neighbors who knew and played with and against the Stanczaks.

Colored House of David　　　　　Washington Stars　　　　　Indianapolis A. B. C's
Lancaster Red Roses　　　　　　Anthracite Miners　　　　　Zulu Jungle Giants
　　　　　　　　　　　　　　　Boston Royal Giants

AL KAHLAU
Sporting Enterprises
2821 Orthodox Street
PHILADELPHIA, PA.

March 1, 1936

Dear Manager:

　　　　Does your club expect to enter the National Championshop Semi-Pro Tournament to be held at Wichita, Kansas? If so I am in a position to book your club towards this City in time to enter same.

　　　　Can also offer your club a 30 day tour in Canada. Your club would be booked for 45 games to be played in 30 days time. Games would be scheduled in the Provinces of Manitoba, Sask., and Alta. Your first game would be scheduled with the Regina, Sask. Club.

　　　　In entering Canada your club would be forced to post $250 with the immigration authorities. This returned to the club when leaving the country.

　　　　Our booking charges are 10%.

　　　　All clubs desiring to have the writer book them must deposit at least $15 advance booking fees as a matter of good faith. This amount is to be deducted from the commissions as they are forwarded to the office.

　　　　At the present time, I have the following clubs lined up to make this Canadian tour. They are as follows, namely, Wichita Eagles formerly Memphis Red Sox, Indianapolis A. B. C's and the Boston Royal Giants.

　　　　Trusting to receive a favorable reply in the very near future, I remain

　　　　Very truly yours,

　　　　Al Kahlau

To my knowledge, though, nobody has recorded the details of the team that set the gold standard for the all-brother teams that proliferated during the Depression. That is what I set out to do. In researching and writing this book I learned so much that was never really discussed by my father or any of my uncles. I cannot imagine that they had these experiences in their life, yet rarely talked about their achievements. I heard a story here and there over the years, but I never really had the complete story until I set out to write this book.

I must admit that when I sat down to write this story, I wondered who would be interested. The longer I worked on the project, however, the more I came to appreciate that this is more than just a story about baseball exploits, though it is most certainly that. Rather, it is a saga of immigration, privation, family bonding, and a father's guiding hand; all topped off by the remarkable accomplishments of ten brothers, both on and off the field. I finish with a tremendous sense of pride in both their baseball prowess and their achievements as brothers, sons, husbands, and fathers.

The last brother died on June 17, 2004, at the age of 93. He is probably playing baseball in the great beyond with his other nine brothers as the best all-brothers team in their new home.

I hope that you will enjoy this short history of an American baseball family as much as I enjoyed researching and writing about them.

Chapter 1
A NEW LIFE IN AMERICA

It all started when a young Martin Stanczak and a friend were walking home one early evening after a few beers at a local tavern in the town of Lapsze Wyzne, Slovakia. The town, then part of the Austro-Hungarian Empire and now in Poland, was where Wojciech Stanczak, Martin's father, sought refuge after fleeing an uprising in Warsaw. While returning home that evening, Martin and his friend crossed the property of a nobleman who chased them down astride a horse, striking them with his riding crop. In defense, Martin and his friend struck back at their assailant. That, of course, was a dangerous transgression in those days. In fear of their lives, they were encouraged to leave the country; and so, Martin and his wife Mary departed for America in 1893 to begin a new chapter.

Upon emigrating to the United States, he was drawn to Chicago, a magnet for newly arrived Poles. Indeed, at one time Chicago had a larger Polish population than Warsaw, the Polish capital.

It was quickly evident to Martin and Mary that Chicago's hustle and bustle was not the place they wanted to raise their family. They soon moved about 50 miles north to the small town of North Chicago, eventually settling on the property that became the family farm. The property was located in the northernmost part of North Chicago, a stone's throw from the City of Waukegan, both located in Lake County hard against the western shores of Lake Michigan.

Years later, this area produced a bounty of fine athletes, many of whom played with and against the brothers Stanczak. Lake County was a hotbed for baseball and sent a host of talent to the minor leagues, including several players who opposed the Stanczak Brothers while playing semi-pro ball. Waukegan produced several major leaguers as well, including Bob O'Farrell, a 21-year veteran catcher, and Johnny Dickshot, who played in the majors from 1936 to 1945. Dickshot played against the Stanczak Brothers as a member of the Knights of Lithuania team. One very notable major leaguer – Bob Feller – married a Waukegan girl while stationed at the Great Lakes Naval Training Station (GLNTS) adjacent to North Chicago. While stationed there during the Second World War he played for GLNTS, a subject that I will touch on later in the story. Otto Graham, another Waukegan native, now enshrined in the Pro Football Hall of Fame, was an All-American quarterback for Northwestern University in Evanston, Illinois, and later a star quarterback for the Chicago Bears.

Waukegan and North Chicago at that time were small microcosms of Europe. The north side of North Chicago was dominated by a strong Irish influence. On the south side, where Martin and Mary had settled, the inhabitants were predominately of Polish descent. Astride Tenth Street, the dividing line between the two cities, were the Slovenians. Traveling north into Waukegan was a neighborhood of Lithuanians. Further north were the Germans. Finally, in the northernmost part of Waukegan was another group of Irishmen, more sophisticated and less rowdy than their countrymen living to the south in North Chicago. Each area had its own church, a large Catholic population, and its own baseball team.

The Italians had settled in Highwood, Illinois, a town about 25 miles south of North Chicago. Highwood was known for producing a great number of talented baseball players. One fellow, Geno "Squeaky" Melchiorre, played shortstop for the St. Joe's Athletic Club, comprised mostly of Poles from North Chicago. "Squeaky" played basketball for Bradley University in Peoria, Illinois and starred as a shortstop on the 1950 Bradley baseball team that represented Bradley University in the College World Series in Omaha, Nebraska.

So, it was this little country town that was to become home to the family. It did not boast any mountains, like the beautiful Carpathian Mountain range that young Martin's birthplace offered, but life was much quieter and more peaceful than Chicago. It was definitely a change from being a "Highlander," as people from his region in Europe were called, but it did offer a serenity of a sort that best suited the life of Martin and Mary Stanczak.

The farm, as it came to be known, was not a large tract of land, but sizable enough to meet their needs. They kept a few dairy cows, from which the family secured its milk, some chickens for the Sunday dinner feasts, and a garden plot where Martin raised the vegetables that sustained the growing family. In addition to his responsibilities on the farm, Martin worked as a molder at the Chicago Hardware Foundry where he was employed for a good part of his life.

Chapter 2
A BASEBALL TEAM IS BORN

Babies started arriving at a pace of about one every two years, beginning in 1895. Eventually it became necessary to move into a larger home able to accommodate the growing brood; thus, a move into the city proper was the next step. The farm was retained and continued to be a source of the family's food. It was in this new home that the boys grew and matured. While father Martin kept the boys busy with farm chores and some coaching, mother Mary was an iron fisted, diminutive housewife who expected – and received – respect and observance of all her demands for housekeeping, cleanliness, studies and religious obligations.

She was only about 4 feet 11 inches tall, but she commanded the respect of a drill sergeant. It may have been a necessary trait given the size of the family and the rapidity at which they arrived. She was a force to be reckoned with when it came to discipline, manners and civil relations between and among family members. She was also the best cook and baker a husband and band of hungry boys could have hoped for. You could set your clock each morning by her daily trip to morning mass. It was no surprise that one of her ten sons would one day enter the seminary and become a priest.

The boys grew in stature physically, as well as in ability. Martin molded each one into a model player for a future baseball team. It was a dream team, the one he fathered, the one he coached over the years, and finally the one where he could put ten of his own sons into baseball uniforms and call them the Stanczak All-Brothers Baseball Team.

The daily routine was Martin at the foundry, the boys in school, followed by completing the daily chores and, of course, practicing the art of baseball. It was a good mix of work and fun for everybody, especially for a proud Martin who was continuously scheduling practices, emphasizing physical training, and developing the boys mentally in the fine points of the game.

Martin, all of 5 feet 7 inches, was a soft-spoken gentleman, but a motivated task master and he saw to it that the boys focused on their physical development. I remember visiting with my grandparents and seeing the crude equipment Martin had improvised for the boys' training needs. There were homemade dummies for lifting and improving arm strength, and a pulley and weight system to build strength and tone their back and stomach muscles.

Needing a place to play ball, they found a nearby empty field on which to practice that became known as Stanczak's Field. This continued for years and along the way additional members were added to the team with each new birth. By the mid-1910's, the older brothers were already playing sandlot ball and had joined some of the local teams. At that time there were numerous sandlot teams in the surrounding area.

When Bill, the second oldest Stanczak son, started throwing a baseball, Martin knew immediately he had found his starting pitcher. My father, John, the eldest brother, took over the warm-up catching job from father Martin because he couldn't handle Bill's heat or Bill's most elusive pitch, which derived its movement from a substance called Slippery Elm chewing tobacco. Bill, who reminded folks of the actor Wallace Berry in both his speech and burly build, mastered the spitball to the extent that it was almost magic, according to John. Making it even harder on the hitters, John claims

John R. Stanczak

Bill threw a "heavy ball," which made it difficult for hitters to launch the ball for long distances.

Chapter 3

WAR COMES TO NORTH CHICAGO

Meanwhile, trouble was brewing in Europe. World War I began on July 28, 1914, and on April 6, 1917, the United States entered the war. Both before and during the war, young men were enlisting and being drafted into service. A considerable number of Major Leaguers joined the armed forces and many of them were sent to the Great Lakes Naval Training Station (GLNTS) located adjacent to North Chicago. It proved to be very fortunate for local baseball talent, who got the opportunity to play on teams selected to play against the GLNTS baseball teams.

World War I and World War II, as well as the Korean Conflict, significantly affected the national pastime during each of the conflicts. During World War I, the minor leagues were shut down and the Major League schedule was shortened. The major leagues continued play during World War II, but the ranks were depleted by the departure of over 500 players who served in the military, including such greats as Ted Williams, Stan Musial, Hank Greenberg, Bob

Feller, and Joe Di Maggio. In addition, thousands of minor leaguers also served.

My father, John, served as a seaman at GLNTS during World War I when the base was struck by the Spanish Flu. The Spanish Flu swept through the ranks and over a two-month period accounted for twice as many deaths at the base as the total number of Americans killed in combat during the entire First World War. Fortunately, John was not among the victims of the pandemic.

The proximity of GLNTS to the home of the Stanczak brothers presented an opportunity to meet and play against many of the major leaguers stationed there. Bill pitched a game in 1917 against future hall-of-famer Red Faber, recording the win by a score of 3-1 in a game in which both pitchers went 17 innings. The game, featuring two dominant spitball hurlers, was tied at one apiece when Bill stepped to the plate in the bottom of the 17th inning and swatted a walk-off home run (I have no record of a scoresheet, or an article which showed a scoresheet for verification; I only have my father's account as to how the game ended).

After that game, Bill was sought out by several Major League scouts, but he refused to sign a contract. Bill wanted to join the Navy and help defeat the Germans who warred on his parent's native country of Poland. The Navy refused his enlistment on account of his young age. Undeterred, with the help of a Polish organization in Chicago, Bill was able to successfully enlist in the Blue Army, composed of Poles fighting with the Allies in France. Before enlisting, Bill played in several other games against teams from GLNTS and on another occasion beat a group of Great Lakes All-Stars by a score of 2-1. With the talent pool available from the minors at that time, the All-Stars comprised a very elite squad of ballplayers.

At the conclusion of the war, Red Faber, the naval pitcher outdueled by Bill in the 17-inning marathon, went back to doing what he did best, pitching in the Major Leagues. And pitch he did, for a total of 4,086 innings, with 1,471 strikeouts and a career ERA of 3.15. In 1954, Red Faber, the last legal spitballer in the majors, was elected to the Baseball Hall of Fame in Cooperstown, a place where a picture of the Stanczak All-Brothers Baseball Team was also prominently displayed.

Bill returned home from his stint with the Blue Army with a shrapnel wound to his head that left a visible scar across his face. He did not play ball for a while, returning to the game only in 1922, at the age of 25. He did pitch again, and he soon showed the form of his pre-war performances.

The decision to join the Blue Army, resulting in a serious injury, and walk away from several serious offers from big league scouts probably deprived Bill of a fine Major League career. He pitched at a Major League caliber level, as proven in his performance against major league stalwart Red Faber. Bill's bat showed flashes of lightning that he displayed on many occasions when he garnered multiple hits and unloaded on pitches for prodigious launches. But Bill had his priorities.

John R. Stanczak

Some Reminisces about World War II's Impact on Local Baseball

After the December 7, 1941 attack on Pearl Harbor, and the swift declaration of war against Japan on December 8th, mobilization began in full swing. This period greatly affected Major League baseball, as well as the minor leagues, and saw an influx of current and future major leaguers pour into Great Lakes Naval Training Station (GLNTS). Mickey Cochrane, former Tigers star catcher and manager, was given the assignment of Supervising Officer in Charge of Athletes at GLNTS; a formidable task that he accepted and performed brilliantly. He had more than 100,000 sailors at his disposal, from which he built the greatest baseball team of all; a team that recorded 188 wins and 32 losses. GLNTS had over 800 baseball teams on base during this period.

The war saw Stanczak brothers Bruno and Julius enter the service, with Julius, an inductee in the latter part of the war, ending up at GLNTS. Bruno, an attorney in private life, was assigned various duties while in the Navy. After several of the games played between Johnson Motors, a team sponsored by a local manufacturing company, and one of the Navy teams, I was privileged to meet several of the players from both teams. Each of the teams had plenty of talent to go around. Among the major leaguers playing at that time were names such as Phil (Scooter) Rizzuto, Peewee Reese, Bob Feller, Johnny Mize, and many others. The one that stood out the most to me was Mickey Cochrane, who was nicknamed "Black Mike." He was a career .320 hitter with 119 homeruns in his major league career. He was very outgoing and friendly. With him around, there were very few dull moments.

My boyhood team, the St. Joe Juniors, were given the uniforms from that fabulous Navy team. The tag in my uniform bore the name of Rizzuto, while my friend, Tony Urbanik, had garnered the uniform worn by Johnny "Big Jawn" Mize, two recognizable Hall-of-Famers.

I suspect a significant percentage of that team ended up as Hall-of-Famers, because a few of the other players among them were Frankie Pytlak and Dom DiMaggio, not to mention many others with similar pedigrees. I felt extremely lucky to have had the opportunity to have been in the company of some of the greatest ballplayers of all times.

In one memorable game between a team sponsored by Waukegan-based Johnson Motors and the GLNTS team, I had the pleasure of seeing my Uncle Marty hit a double off a pitch from "Schoolboy" Rowe – a three-time Major League All-Star who pitched on three Tigers' World Series teams – right after Rowe struck out a string of Johnson Motors batters. Another thrill was seeing Marty launch a

Bob Feller fastball that carried out of the ballfield, over the running track, and over the fence of the football field at Weiss Field in Waukegan. I am quite sure it traveled a good 400 feet.

The Johnson Motors team for which brothers Marty and Louis both played into the 1940's was comprised of many ex-minor leaguers who had returned home after leaving organized baseball in the 1930's, mainly because of the Depression. There were players like Lefty Nelson, who was forced to quit professionally after putting his fist through a window during a dream one night, Orville Baker, Duke Alto, Bud Hubley and George Vavrek, among other very talented players.

Chapter 4.

BACK TO BASEBALL

As time went by, additional brothers joined the family, and eventually there was the makings of a baseball team with ages ranging from 14 to 33. For several years, the question pervaded Martin Sr.'s mind: When can or should we start playing as an all-brothers baseball team? Time was flying by, and the answer had to come sooner rather than later. On a spring morning in 1928, he felt the question needed to be broached and decided to get the boys together to finalize the decision. He told the boys that he felt the time had come to play as an all-brothers team, as the age difference among the boys left a very narrow window for this to become a reality. He thought that the younger brothers could learn while they played, fearing the older brothers would begin to age out of the game. It was inevitable from his perspective that his dream of many years, an all-brothers team, would come to fruition.

The boys were surprised to learn that the team would start playing that summer. A minor "insurrection" was brewing among the older boys because they were already playing with, and competing against, seasoned ballplayers on winning teams, such as Kiejko's Colts and Killians Plumbing.

They voiced concerns about winning on an all-brothers team that included 14-year-old Julius and 18-year-old Martin, Jr., both of whom were untested and inexperienced.

Martin, Sr. poses with several of his boys and their teammates during their Killians Plumbing playing days.

To move his plans forward, Martin Sr. responded with rhetorical questions:

- "Are you older brothers not good enough at the game to overcome a few errors that may be encountered at the outset?"

- "What are you made of that you cannot see that this could be a great team?"

- "Are you not capable of lifting one another up if the situation calls for it?"

He followed these questions with recommendations to improve his son's skills and for the team as a whole:

- "Bill and Michael, you have to be more focused on the mound when pitching."

- "Eddie, Joe, Frank, pick it up a notch and get your batting eyes sharpened."

- "All of you as a team have to get defensively stronger to be in the winner's circle."

He neither commanded nor demanded that the boys acquiesce to his dream of forming an all-brothers team, but they knew by the tenor of their father's voice that they would submit to his wishes. The challenge was accepted by everyone, and the Stanczak's All-Brothers Baseball Team was officially born.

The author's father, John (front, right),
posing with teammates from the Kiejko Colts.

Meet the Team

The time has come to get to know these boys of summer from Lake County, Illinois. Introducing them by order of birth (from left to right in the photo above) we start with John (Mush), Bill, Joe (Curly), Frank (Fry Cake), Mike, Ed, Bruno (Moon), Louis (Kibby), Martin (Sniffer), Julius (Zeke):

John (Mush) – My father, he worked at the corner bakery as a young man; from there to the foundry; opened a barber shop; and eventually built the first bowling alley in North Chicago. He lost the bowling alley during the Great Depression but was able to claim it back and ultimately turned the business over to his youngest son, Jim. John fathered nine children of his own and at the time of his death he had 29 great grandchildren.

Bill – Refused offers from several major league teams after defeating Red Faber, who was playing with the Great Lakes All-Stars, and, instead, enlisted to fight with the Poles in the Blue Army in World War I. Bill was the star of the team and accounted for many victories. Bill was sometimes called the "Iron Man McGinnity" of the Stanczak team. Like the original bearer of that name, Joseph Jerome "Iron Man" McGinnity – who often pitched both games of doubleheaders as a member of the New York Giants – Bill pitched back-to-back games on numerous occasions.

Joe (Curly) – Spent 38 years of his working life in public service, mostly as the City Tax Collector and also as a Deputy County Clerk. He and brother Eddie started up the City Cab Company, which they sold when they both retired. Joe played in the minors, but I could not find any information regarding his affiliations.

Frank (Fry Cake) – Like two of his other brothers, played with several minor league baseball teams in his early years. He played in the Florida State League and in the American Association with the Milwaukee Brewers. His career ended due to a broken leg suffered at spring training camp with the Pittsburgh Pirates.

Mike (Father Mike) – Studied for the priesthood at St. Mary of the Lake Seminary in Mundelein, Illinois, which he paid for out of his baseball earnings, while still playing with the All-Brothers team. While preparing for the priesthood in 1929, he stroked a double that proved to be the winning run in a very contentious ballgame; causing him to miss his ordination. He was ordained into the priesthood in 1930 and continued to play when his church duties permitted. He celebrated his 50th anniversary as a priest in June 1980, at Holy Rosary Church in North Chicago, where he attended mass during his childhood days.

Ed – Spent most of his life as a barber in North Chicago, and at Great Lakes Naval Training Center where he was a manager for the Navy Exchange in charge of the barber shops. Co-owned the City Cab Company with Joe. Eddie, too, was an outstanding ballplayer. He was signed by the Milwaukee Brewers of the American Association but was unable to continue due to an arm injury. Eddie also turned down several other offers to play minor league baseball.

Bruno (Moon) – Attended Archbishop Quigley Preparatory Seminary, went onto St. Bede's College, and studied law at Loyola University. He practiced law in North Chicago, was elected Police Magistrate and eventually elected the State's Attorney for Lake County, Illinois. While serving in that capacity he was responsible for having the salacious book "Deep Throat" removed from the shelves of all stores in Lake County. While serving in the Navy during WW II (after receiving his Naval Officer Training at Princeton University), Bruno was assigned to a special group investigating the facilities in midwestern colleges for possible attendance by Naval personnel. He attended gunnery training at Fort Davis in North Carolina. He was stationed at Pacific Beach serving as an anti-aircraft instructor for a six-month period in 1943. His last assignment was as captain of an LST just prior to the end of the war.

Louis (Kibby) – A very good defensive catcher with an excellent arm, and a consistent bat handler. He was destined to play baseball and did so in the minor leagues, most notably with a call up to the Milwaukee Brewers and attendance at spring training with the Cincinnati Reds at the age of 17. Baseball players at that time were not being paid much money, and travel and eating conditions were not very favorable. He, like his brothers Marty and Frank, ended up working and playing baseball for Johnson Motors, a manufacturer of outboard motors in Waukegan, Illinois. He ended his working days with them.

Marty (Sniffer) – Like brothers Frank and Louis, he was a very talented outfielder with a rifle arm, above average defensive ability, and a consistent hitter with dangerous power. He had several minor league stints, played in the Nebraska State League, and attended spring training with the Cincinnati Reds before leaving pro ball to work and play for Johnson Motors.

Julius – The youngest of the brothers, he entered into the work force as an auto mechanic, later serviced the City Cab autos for his older brothers, and eventually owned and operated the City Garage in North Chicago. He later became parts manager for a local automobile dealer, a job from which he retired.

All of the brothers enjoyed a long life, with four of the ten living past the age of 90, three into their 80's, and two into their 70's. Only one brother, Louis, passed at an early age.

Brothers	Year of Birth	Year of Death	Age at Death
John	1895	1988	92
Bill	1897	1991	93
Joe	1901	1986	85
Frank	1902	1979	77
Mike	1904	1989	85
Eddie	1906	1996	90
Bruno	1907	1977	70
Louis	1910	1963	53
Marty	1912	2004	92
Julius	1914	2001	87

Parents	Year of Birth	Year of Death	Age at Death
Martin, Sr.	1873	1957	74
Mary	1873	1965	91

From then on it was practice, practice, practice, every time the opportunity arose. It was sliding into second or home plate; throws from the outfield into the bases; infield practice; working on the art of completing the double play; and anything else it took to mold a team.

They weren't major leaguers, but they knew how to play the game and they gained the reputation as the team to beat. Their prowess was not only recognized in the Lake County area, but everywhere from Chicago to Milwaukee. This was not just any ordinary sandlot team; it was an organization with a secretary, Joe "Curly" Stanczak, who managed all the bookings, arranged the schedule, and promoted games with different organizations, especially the National Semi-Pro Baseball Congress. Indeed, Joe was selected for the position of District Commissioner for the National Semi-Pro Baseball Congress.

They played games as both the "Stanczak All-Brothers" team and the "Stanczak Brothers" team. When they played as the Stanczak All-Brothers team, every one of the ten siblings was on the roster. The latter name was used in the later years when other players were substituted into the line-up as the older brothers began to leave the game or when one or more of the brothers had to tend to other responsibilities. For instance, Mike had his priestly obligations and John was a business owner who needed to focus on other matters of importance.

The Stanczak Brothers Team with a
mixture of brothers and others.

> ### *What's in a Name?*
>
> Oddly enough, there are numerous pictures of the team with the name "STANZAK" sprawled across their uniforms. There are several different stories as to why the letter "c" was left out of the team name. One story is that the correctly spelled name would not fit on the uniform. Another version claims that omitting the "c" helped announcers properly pronounce the family's name. Yet another tale is that it was simply a spelling error when the uniforms were produced, though that is unlikely given that the "abbreviated" name appeared on several iterations of the team's uniform.
>
>

Throughout its existence, the team had numerous offers to play games scheduled in other states by Sporting Enterprises of Philadelphia, Pennsylvania, including a semi-pro tournament in Wichita, Kansas, and another opportunity to participate in a tournament in Canada comprising 45 games to be played over a 30-day period across three provinces. One offer, received in 1929, was to play a team in Milwaukee, Wisconsin for a guaranteed $900 purse.

That offer was refused for fear that one of the boys would get injured, handicapping them in their upcoming All-Brothers Championship Series against the Marlatt Brothers of Wyoming. John broke his leg sliding into second base in a game prior to another important series and the team did not want to risk a repeat of that mishap. Nine hundred dollars was a lot of money in those Great Depression days, but a shot at the "national championship" carried more cachet in the grand scheme of things.

Throughout this period, the brothers played a lot of baseball, coalescing into a strong team. They traveled to many different states as part of their association with the National Semi-Pro Baseball Congress (NSPBC), including Alabama, Kansas, Nebraska, Texas, Wisconsin, and Wyoming, not to mention Canada.

Stories about the brothers appeared in newspapers across the country. Throughout my research, I frequently came across articles portraying the team as a group of solidly proficient ballplayers worthy of the many accolades that were heaped upon them. It is apparent that they played consistently good defensive baseball; and in addition, they were all accomplished hitters. The big sticks among the older brothers were Bill, Frank and Mike, while the younger group consisted of Bruno, Louis and Martin. I single them out because, unlike Joe (Curly) and Eddie, who consistently hit for average, those six had some explosive thunder in their bats and could unload on a pitcher for those triples and homers that are the coveted crown jewels of baseball.

To put it succinctly, they were a force to be reckoned with and were viewed as fierce competitors and worthy opponents by all they faced. There was not a weak spot in the line-up; never allowing opposing pitchers any opportunity to let up. It is worth noting, however, that pitching – particularly Bill's pitching – played a significant role in the team's overall success.

In both local and out-of-state games, they encountered stars of the game, including Satchel Paige (Kansas City Monarchs) while playing in Wichita, Kansas at an NSPBC tournament; and Lou Boudreau in Harvey, Illinois while playing within the Chicago-Milwaukee region. The same happened on a more local basis, where players with exceptional talent, such as John Dickshot of the Knights of Lithuania, were playing prior to being called up to the "Show." There was no shortage of exceptional players available during their playing years and the brothers fared well while competing against any number of celebrated players.

Chapter 5
A WORLD CHAMPIONSHIP

It was 1929 when the brothers started playing competitively as an all-brothers team. That was the year that Julius, the youngest brother, celebrated his 15th birthday. By that point, he had reached a level of proficiency that allowed the team to use him as a substitute when the need arose. Julius, like every other member of the team, had to be versatile and learn to play different positions. He eventually played the role of utility outfielder, as well as infielder, and was even called on to pitch occasionally. The only two positions consistently held by the same players were second base, with Curly manning that spot, and first base where Eddie was the mainstay. Needless to say, fielding a team consisting of ten players – all brothers – necessitated versatility.

The team caught the eye of a respected local political figure, Nick Keller. He arranged a game between the Stanczak All-Brothers Baseball Team and the Marlatt Brothers of Hawk Springs, Wyoming, another all-brothers team that he learned of through a coffee salesman that did business with the Marlatt Brothers. The two envisioned the series as an All-Brothers World Series between two evenly matched teams. So, in 1929, a challenge was issued to the Stanczak Brothers to play the Marlatt Brothers for the All-Brothers World Championship in a best of seven series to be played between Cheyenne, Wyoming and Waukegan, Illinois. The Stanczak All-Brothers Baseball Team accepted the challenge.

The Marlatt Brothers, together with the Stanczaks, were among the 24 known brothers' teams in baseball history. They too accepted the challenge to play for the right to claim the title of "World's All-Brothers Baseball Champions." The Marlatt Brothers ranged in age from 17 to 45 years old, while the Stanczak Brothers were fielding a team that featured players from 15 to 33 years of age. Some of the Marlatts formed the nucleus of the Hawk Springs Baseball Club, which was contending for the North Platte Valley League Championship just prior to the Marlatts traveling to Cheyenne for the first game of the seven-game series. In the All-Brothers World Championship series, the Marlatt Brothers sported uniforms they had purchased (though some reports claim they were rented or borrowed) from the Chicago White Sox, which still displayed the Sox emblem.

As the first series of the game approached, the Stanczak Brothers, decked out in their Sunday best, excitedly boarded a bus for Cheyenne, Wyoming. Martin and Mary, their proud parents, and Nick Keller accompanied the team. The trio formed the entire contingent of Stanczak Brothers' fans among the crowd of Marlatt boosters who were there to cheer the home team onto victory.

Setting off for the All-Brothers World Championship Series in 1929.

The first two games were played in Cheyenne, Wyoming. The opener was played on Saturday, August 24, 1929, with the first pitch being thrown out by Wyoming Governor Frank C. Emerson. Frank, the leadoff hitter for the Stanczak Brothers, had a high average coupled with long ball power. Joe and Eddie, numbers two and three in the order, were consistent hitters, with Eddie flashing power from time to time. Bill, the "Iron Man McGinnity" of the Stanczak clan, was the clean-up hitter, a rarity for a pitcher; but he had the power. Bruno, batter number five, mixed average with power. Next up were Louis and then Marty. They were both excellent hitters. John and Julius brought up the eighth and ninth spots in the batting order. This formidable Stanczak lineup kept the Marlatts' pitchers on their toes throughout the game.

The Game One lineup is shown below:

STANCZAK BROTHERS		MARLATT BROTHERS	
Frank	Shortstop	Bryan	Catcher, Shortstop
Joe	2nd Base	Ray	2nd Base
Eddie	1st Base	Ed	3rd Base
Bill	Pitcher	Lloyd	1st Base
Bruno	Centerfield	Glenn	Centerfield, Catcher
Louis	Catcher	Jack	Pitcher, Centerfield
Martin	Rightfield	Erwin	Shortstop, Pitcher
John	Shortstop	Bill	Rightfield
Julius	Leftfield	Ernest	Leftfield
		Ray	Leftfield

Father Mike was not in the series-opener line-up card for unknown reasons; but it is likely he was performing his priestly duties (maybe praying for a Stanczak Brothers' victory in the process).

In the first contest, won by the Stanczak Brothers, the crowd was treated to an offensive display that featured three home runs as part of a 12-hit barrage by the Stanczak team, while the Marlatts out-hit the Stanczaks with 14 of their own. A strong defensive game by the Stanczaks kept the scoring damage to a minimum and the Stanczaks walked off the field with an 11-5 victory, putting them one game up in the best-of-seven series.

| **GAME 1 BOX SCORE** | | | | |

STANCZAK BROTHERS		AB	R	H
Frank	Shortstop	4	2	1
Joe	2nd Base	4	2	1
Eddie	1st Base	4	2	1
Bill	Pitcher	5	2	3
Bruno	Leftfield	4	1	1
Louis	Center	5	0	2
Martin	Rightfield	5	1	1
John	3rd Base	5	0	0
Julius	Leftfielder	5	1	2

MARLATT BROTHERS		AB	R	H
Bryan	Catcher, Shortstop	5	1	1
Ray	2nd Base	5	0	0
Ed	3rd Base	4	2	3
Lloyd	1st Base	4	0	0
Glenn	Centerfield, Catcher	4	1	2
Jack	Pitcher, Centerfield	4	0	2
Ervin	Shortstop, Pitcher	4	0	2
Bill	Rightfield	4	0	2
Ernest	Leftfield	2	0	1
Ray	Leftfield	2	1	1

The Sunday game started out rocky for the visiting Stanczaks. Their starting pitcher, Marty, gave up three hits, including a two-run homer by Ray Marlatt in the 2nd inning.

Trailing by three runs with nobody out, Bill entered the game in relief of Marty. This followed Bill's complete-game victory the prior day, once again demonstrating why he deserved the "Iron Man McGinnity" appellation. Bill stifled the Marlatts by surrendering only five hits and allowing two runs through the remaining innings, going the distance.

Game Two was another defensive gem for the Stanczaks, featuring four double-plays. Their defensive ability eliminated base runners and kept the Marlatts' scoring in check. It was a combination of pitching, offense and defense that culminated in a come-from-behind 8-5 victory.

With the Stanczaks leading the series by two games to none, play resumed on Saturday, September 28th, with Game Three played at Weiss Field in Waukegan, Illinois. Game Three was won by the Stanczak brothers, but I could not locate any records with the details of that game.

In the final game of the series, played the next day, the crowd was treated to a low scoring affair featuring solid pitching on both sides. There was a little hiccup on the part of the Marlatt pitcher in the first inning: a pair of walks, a single, and an error permitted two Stanczak Brothers' runs to score. The rest of the game featured solid pitching, holding each team to only one more run. Bill pitched a complete-game two-hitter, while striking out four and issuing no walks. The Stanczak All-Brothers Baseball Team claimed the title of "All-Brothers Baseball World Champs!"

Interestingly, one newspaper reported that six games were played in the seven-game series. According to that article, two games were played in Cheyenne, and four were played in Waukegan, the last two being exhibition games.

John R. Stanczak

Although the number of games differed, the outcome was the same: The Stanczak Brothers won them all.

Chapter 6

IT AINT OVER TILL THE FAT LADY SINGS

The Stanczaks played as the Stanczak All-Brothers Baseball Team from 1929 until 1936. After age caught up with several of them, the younger brothers took the field under the "Stanczak Brothers" banner; still consisting primarily of brothers with a few other players with exceptional credentials recruited to fill out the team. They continued to play for several more years until the last two brothers, still active, started playing for the Johnson Motors team to finish out their baseball days.

In 1935, the Stanczak Brothers received another challenge from a group of brothers located in Hye, Texas: the Diekes. The Dieke Brothers were considered the better of the two teams, but they too fell to the Stanczaks by a score of 11-5. According to some sources, the Dieke's played a ringer in this game: the future 36th President of the United States was said to be their first baseman on that day. Word had it that Lyndon Johnson was a smooth fielding first baseman and a dangerous hitter. Whether true or not, it is known that LBJ played on at least one occasion with the Dieke Brothers.

Though the glory days ultimately ended, the brothers left behind a legacy that will never be matched. One cannot help but wonder how things might have been different had Bill accepted one of the Major League offers after beating Red Farber in 1917. There is little doubt that Bill could have competed at the Major League level with his wicked spitball and a pitch termed as a "heavy ball." Had that happened though, the Stanczak All-Brothers World Champions might never have existed. Bill was responsible for many of the team's victories and most stories about the team lauded him as a superb competitor. The ultimate compliment, however, came from his siblings, who acclaimed him the team hero. As it was, this band of brothers lived long and enviable lives, travelling and playing together and excelling at the great American pastime, and then going on to live full and happy lives making numerous contributions to their communities.

The brothers celebrate Father Mike's 50th anniversary as a priest.

Some Career Highlights

- All-Brothers World Championship Series (1929) –
  - Wyoming Governor Frank Emerson throws out the first pitch to start the series.
  - Bill pitches back-to-back games, winning the first contest on Saturday 11-5, and the second game on Sunday 8-5 after coming on in relief in the second inning.
  - Eddie finished the second game with a homerun and three singles for a 4-for-5 day at-bat.
  - Defensively, the Stanczaks turned four double plays in the second game.
  - Several newsreel cameramen recorded the events for the new "talking pictures" medium. (This can be viewed on clips featured on Getty Images https://www.gettyimages.com/detail/video/baseballs-all-in-family-here-waukegan-ill-two-brother-news-footage/825016718.)

- Lake County Championship Series (1931) –
  - Bill pitches a double-header against St. Anthony's, winning the first game 20-11 while giving up 10 hits.

- Bill wins the second contest by a score of 7-3, pitching a three-hitter.
- Frank, Marty and Bruno each homer in the first game as the team garners 25 hits against the ace pitcher of the Saints, "Zaits" Navickus.

- National Semi-Pro Tournament in Wichita, Kansas (1935) –
  - In the feature game of the tournament, the Stanczak Brothers beat another "all-brothers" team, the Deikes, from Hye, Texas, by a score of 11-5.

- National Semi-Pro Game in Wichita, Kansas (1935) –
  - Frank homers in the 4th inning as the brothers beat the Japanese All-Stars 5-4. In addition to this homer, Frank pounded out a double and a single for a 3-for-4 day at bat, with Bruno adding a double.

- Lake County Championship Game (1933) –
  - A crowd of 1,200 is on hand to watch the boys defeat the vaunted Knights of Lithuania.

- Louie goes 3-for-4, while Eddie goes 3-for-3, all part of a 13-hit attack that propelled them to a 7-6 victory.

- Lake County Championship (1934) –
    - Bill pitches a one hit ballgame in a win against the Knights of Lithuania.
    - Played against the W.C. Morrison team in the final game.

- Lake County Championship (1935)
    - Late inning batting heroics by Eddie and Louie saved the game and gave the Stanczak Brothers the title that year.

- Other Memorable Moments –
    - The brothers defeat the Poplar Bluff, Missouri team (Missouri State Champs) before being eliminated by the Denver Fuel (Colorado State Champs) by the score of 5-4 in a 10-inning duel.
    - Mike Stanczak pitches an eight hit, 3-1 victory, over the Great Lakes (GLNTS) All Stars. Frank delivers a triple, while brother Joe chips in with a double.
    - Bill pitches a seven-hitter against Killians Plumbing. Mike triples, Bruno doubles, and Marty, Frank, and Bill single, which

> spells victory by the score of 11-7 over the Old-Timers.
> - Bill strikes out 11 batters, walks one, in a 2-1 victory over a powerful McHenry team that outhit the brothers 9-to-7, in a game featuring a spectacular running catch in left centerfield by John in the bottom of the 12th inning to save the day.
>
> • Playing as the all-brothers team, the Stanczak Brothers compiled an enviable seven-year record of 115 wins and 31 losses for a .780-win percentage –
>   - The best year was 1932, when they finished with 25 wins against only three losses.
>   - In 1933, they finished with an 18-and-3 record, the last year they played every game as an all-brothers team.

Appendix
MY BASEBALL MEMORIES

Like my father and uncles, I too loved the game of baseball. Like most boys of my era, I grew up playing sandlot ball in my hometown of North Chicago. I played a little baseball in high school until, ironically, my dad made me quit so I had more time to do chores around the bowling alley. That did not, however, end my playing days. I went on to play several seasons of American Legion baseball before joining the "feeder" squad for a local team fielded by the St. Joe's Athletic Club. Following in the footsteps of my younger uncles, I played several different positions: second base, shortstop, first base and – despite my rather diminutive stature – catcher, when the need arose.

I was playing for the St. Joe's Athletic Club when the Korean Conflict broke out and I enlisted in the Army. I was "lucky" enough to be assigned to Vint Hill Farms Station, a post in Virginia where baseball was a big deal; giving me the opportunity to play with and against some notable athletes. I placed quotes around the word "lucky" because, unfortunately, my baseball career was also ended while playing for my Vint Hill Farms team. While learning the fine points of a new position – third base – I collided violently with our team catcher while attempting to field an infield pop-up. That collision landed me in the hospital for several months with life-threatening injuries.

Sixty-seven years later, my shoulder still throbs from time-to-time, reminding me of that moment. But I do not mind, because that moment was just one of my many baseball memories, most of them wonderful! I have tried to share some of those memories with the readers in the earlier parts of this book and in the pages that follow. I hope you will find as much pleasure in reading these stories as I have experienced in writing about them.

The Rexes
While playing in the North Shore Semi Pro League in Lake County, Illinois, our St. Joe's Juniors team played each of the other teams several times during the baseball season. An African American team called the "Rexes" was outfitted and managed by a prominent Black physician from Waukegan, Illinois, Eugene P. King, M.D. Dr. King was a well-liked and highly respected man and served a vast number of patients in his practice. He apparently was also a dedicated sportsman because he played both baseball and basketball with his sponsored teams. Although he outfitted his teams, the Rexes' catcher never wore protective gear. That was because Dr. King was also the team catcher and he refused to wear any gear. Amazingly, he was in his late forties and early fifties when I played against Dr. King and the Rexes.

It was always a pleasure and a challenge when the schedule pitted us against Rexes. Dr. King was a very talented receiver with a good throwing arm, as well as a .250 to .260 batting average. In all the games we played against the Rexes, not one time did I ever see him get clipped by a foul tip. It was rare for a wild pitch or pass ball to get by him.

To this day I have great admiration for the man he was, as well as for his baseball skills. I can still picture him with pant legs pulled up to the top of his knees, with orange and black baseball stockings being prominently displayed. The young men that he mentored certainly owe a debt of gratitude to a very fine man. He molded them into good sportsmen and, most importantly from his perspective, into upstanding members of the community.

Army Days
As I mentioned earlier, I was stationed at the U.S. Army's Vint Hill Farms Station in Virginia during the Korean Conflict. I had the pleasure of playing on the Post baseball team which was part of the Maisac League in the Military District of Washington, D.C. In one memorable home game, we played a team from Fort Eustis. I cannot recall the final score of the game, but I vividly remember our centerfielder racing with his back to home plate to catch a long drive off the bat of an opposing player from Fort Eustis. Our centerfielder, Harry Brownfield, was a speedster from Uniontown, Pennsylvania, who attended Slippery Rock College and, while there, set a 50-yard dash record in the Drake Relays.

The batter who was "robbed" of an extra base hit by the streaking centerfielder was none other than the great Willie Mays, already a well-known and accomplished hitter playing professional baseball for the New York Giants when drafted into the Army. Willie was left shaking his head as he rounded first base on his way to second. I do believe that Willie went to school on this catch, which he was to replicate in the eighth inning of Game One of the 1954 World Series when his Giants took on the Cleveland Indians. With runners on first and second, Vic Wertz, another speedster, hit a 425-foot shot to centerfield. This time, the guy deprived by Harry Brownfield of an extra base hit turned apparent jubilation into utter disappointment for one Vic Wertz, his Indians' teammates, and Tribe fans everywhere.

After our Army games, it was customary for the two teams to travel to the home team's mess hall for the traditional postgame feast. I guess the four hungriest guys, of which I was one, ended up being first in line for chow. After filling our trays, we raced to the first four seats available and sat down: one, two, three, four. Number four being none other than the "Say Hey Kid," Willie Mays. He was a voracious eater, a great conversationalist (friendly and humorous), and very unpretentious. The dinner I shared with him is certainly high on my list of memorable moments. I fully understand why he was admired by so many fans and players alike.

On another occasion during my stint in the Army, I had the opportunity to go quail hunting with Johnny Klippstein, who played 18 years in the Major Leagues. Johnny was married to my high school friend, Mary Ann Artac, who also happened to be the niece of Dutch Leonard. Dutch was a famous knuckleball pitcher who was playing for the Cubs at the time (1949 – 1953). Johnny was introduced to Mary Ann by his teammate, Dutch, and they ended up getting married in 1951 (they used my parents' home for their pre-wedding preparations).

While visiting Washington, D.C. for a weekend, Johnny and Mary Ann visited me at Vint Hill. Johnny took me quail hunting on his Uncle's farm in Virginia. Result of the quail hunt:

- Quail bagged: 0
- Scratches from the bramble bushes: Multiple

The weekend was a great experience with two exceptional people, now etched in the memory book and filed under "good memories."

In addition to Willie Mays, I had the opportunity to play against several other major and minor leaguers during my Army stint. Among the more notable names were Russ Meyer of the Philadelphia Phillies, Vernon Law and Chet Nichols of the Pittsburgh Pirates, Danny O'Connell of the Milwaukee Braves, and Sam Calderone of the New York Giants.

I have very fond memories of my teammates on the Vint Hill Farms Station team. I already mentioned our speedy centerfielder, Harry Brownfield. Other members of the team included Charlie Yancey (3B), Dick Kirk (LF), Rollie Teater (C), Reinhard "Rex" Heinenger (1B), Cotton Fennel (SS), Dominic Diflorido (2B), Willie Collie (P), Lefty Gould (P), Mel Milender (P), and Bobby Madison (C). Unfortunately, I can no longer remember the name of our right fielder, which is surprising because he was a very good ballplayer and a great guy to boot. All of these players were polished hitters and proficient fielders. I owe a particular debt of gratitude to "Rex" Heinenger, who probably saved my life with his quick reactions following an infield collision during practice that landed me in the hospital for several months.

Lost Opportunity
Let me close with a brief story about "the one that got away." I lived for many years in Paragould, Arkansas, where I owned and operated a group of fast-food restaurants. While living in Paragould, I had the pleasure of befriending Don Williams, a former major league coach and scout for the San Diego Padres and the Atlanta Braves. Don played for many years in the Dodgers' minor league system. He was a close friend of Duke Snyder, long-time, all-star centerfielder for the Brooklyn and Los Angeles Dodgers. Don knew how much I admired Duke and decided to surprise me one day by bringing him by my restaurant to introduce us. To my never-ending dismay, I happened to be out of town that day and missed my opportunity to meet another of the legends of the game. But I am surely grateful to both Don and Duke for thinking of me like that.

ABOUT THE AUTHOR

This story has been waiting a long time to be told. It has been more than 100 years since the first of the Stanczak brothers threw his baseball mitt on the field that became their field of dreams—a cow pasture near the family home. My father, John, Sr., was the oldest brother on the famous Stanczak All-Brothers baseball team. My younger brother Jim and I long planned to collaborate in telling this story. Unfortunately, Jim died in 2018, after compiling much of the historical data about the brothers' story. I regret that Jim and I were unable to finish this labor of love together.

I have waited far too long to record this rich history that honors my father and uncles, and to share their remarkable stories with the current generation. My children and grandchildren and all the descendants of the Stanczak All-Brothers baseball team—indeed anybody who enjoys a good baseball story—deserve to know the true history of ten brothers who left their mark on our great American pastime.

Understandably, baseball was always important in my family when I was growing up. I had tryouts with the Chicago Cubs as a catcher and the Cleveland Indians as

John R. Stanczak

an infielder. I hit a homerun during the Cubs' tryout, but unfortunately it was not enough to earn me a contract. But I had the opportunity to meet several famous ballplayers over the years, and even played against some of them, including the great Willie Mays. I played baseball in the army during the Korean Conflict, until I was seriously injured in a collision with another player while attempting to catch an infield pop-up. That ended my baseball playing days.

Over the years since then, I have been a serial entrepreneur. I owned a bowling alley together with my brother Jim in our hometown of Waukegan, Illinois. Moving on from there, I owned a group of fast-food restaurants in northeast Arkansas, followed by a golf business in Florida, and a window treatment business in Tennessee. I finally retired at the ripe age of 82 and now live in Nashville, Tennessee, with the love of my life. I hope to write more, but having recently celebrated my 90th birthday I know I will have to write fast!

www.ingramcontent.com/pod-product-compliance
Lightning Source LLC
LaVergne TN
LVHW011858060526
838200LV00054B/4413